Creepy Crawlies

Bees

Rebecca Rissman

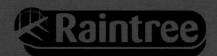

www.raintreepublishers.co.uk
Visit our website to find out
more information about
Raintree books.

To order:
☎ Phone 0845 6044371
🖺 Fax +44 (0) 1865 312263
🖻 Email myorders@raintreepublishers.co.uk

Customers from outside the UK please telephone +44 1865 312262

Raintree is an imprint of Capstone Global Library Limited, a company incorporated in England and Wales having its registered office at 7 Pilgrim Street, London, EC4V 6LB – Registered company number: 6695582

Text © Capstone Global Library Limited 2013
First published in hardback in 2013
Paperback edition first published in 2014
The moral rights of the proprietor have been asserted.

Edited by Dan Nunn, Rebecca Rissman, and Catherine Veitch
Designed by Joanna Hinton-Malivoire
Picture research by Mica Brancic
Originated by Capstone Global Library Ltd
Production by Victoria Fitzgerald
Printed in China by South China Printing Company Ltd

ISBN 978 1 406 24131 0 (hardback)
16 15 14 13 12
10 9 8 7 6 5 4 3 2 1

ISBN 978 1 406 24145 7 (paperback)
17 16 15 14 13
10 9 8 7 6 5 4 3 2 1

British Library Cataloguing in Publication Data
Rissman, Rebecca.
Bees. – (Creepy crawlies)
595.7'99-dc22
A full catalogue record for this book is available from the British Library.

Acknowledgements
We would like to thank the following for permission to reproduce photographs: Dreamstime p. 22 (© Alexey Fedorov); iStockphoto p. 9 (© Antagain); Photoshot pp. 15 (© Biosphoto), 16, 17 (NHPA); Shutterstock pp. 1, 5 (© Vladimir Sazonov), 6 (© Allocricetulus), 7 (© Voyagerix), 10, 11 (© Mircea Bezergheanu), 13 (© IKO), 18 (© Daniel Prudek), 19 (© LilKar), 20 (© Ljupco Smokovski), 21 (© Gherasim Rares), 22 (© Alex Staroseltsev, © alle, © Photolinc, © Tomo Jesenicnik, © Vinicius Tupinamba), 23 (© Ivaschenko Roman, © Jocic, © Péter Gudella, © Vnlit).

Cover photograph of a bumblebee on a flower reproduced with permission of Shutterstock (© Joanna Zopoth-Lipiejko).

Every effort has been made to contact copyright holders of any material reproduced in this book. Any omissions will be rectified in subsequent printings if notice is given to the publisher.

The publishers would like to thank Michael Bright for his assistance in the preparation of this book.

Contents

Let's search!

Do you hear that sound?

Is that a bee over there, with stripes of black and yellow fuzz?

Six little legs help a bee to walk around.

But it's a bee's wings that make that buzzing sound!

wings

Four clear wings help honeybees to fly.
Can you spot the wings on this bee rushing by?

Two big eyes help a bee to look around.

eye

So when
it's flying high,
a bee can see
what's on
the ground!

Bees have stingers too,
which keep enemies away.

It hurts if you're stung, so remember, bees don't like to play!

13

Bees live in hives or nests,
but don't ever go too near.

Because if a bee feels in
danger, it may sting you
out of fear!

Bee eggs grow into larvae.
Larvae are small and white.

Then larvae grow into pupae, and soon the young bees take flight!

pollen

When bees are fully grown, they fly out of their nests.

Collecting pollen and nectar to bring home, trying to do their best.

Do you like eating honey?
It's a tasty treat!

Bees use pollen and nectar to make honeycomb – it's good enough to eat!

Counting bees

Look carefully at these two pages.
How many bees can you see?

Look near the white flowers
and in front of the tree!

Did you know?

Bees see all colours except the colour red.

Index